Diesels Nationwide

Volume Four

DIESELS NATIONWIDE

compiled by Colin Judge

Volume Four

Oxford Publishing Co.

ISBN 0-86093-114-5

Half title page: A Doncaster Works Class 08 shunter, No. 08420, takes a well-earned rest in the Works yard on 3rd September 1978.

Peter Gater

Typesetting by:
Aquarius Typesetting Services, New Milton, Hants.

Printed in Great Britain by:
Biddles Ltd., Guildford, Surrey.

Published by:
Oxford Publishing Co.,
Link House,
West Street, POOLE,
Dorset.

Above: The prototype unit, No. 140001 is pictured at Blackburn, on 23rd September 1981, with a Colne to Preston working during passenger service trials.

Paul Shannon

Frontispiece: Class 37, No. 37055 powers through Welwyn Garden City with 6P36, the 14.13 King's Cross to Cambridge sand empties train, on 25th September 1981.

Paul Shannon

Title page: Two unidentified Class 25 locomotives pass Castleford signal box, in 1974, with a stone train from Rylstone to Hull.

John Glover

Introduction

The preparation of a further volume in the *Diesels Nationwide* series, prompted me to seek new and exciting scenes of British Rail trains in unusual settings, incorporating some from railway photographers whose work is rarely seen. It soon became very obvious that since compiling *Diesels Nationwide (Volume Two)*, many locations, lines and stations seem to have been abandoned, lifted or closed and that the railway system was, again, quietly in decline. I therefore decided to take a look back into the 1970s, in this volume, rather than look at the present day, which, to me, seems to be covered prolifically by the many modern image albums and magazines appearing with monotonous regularity.

For this volume, many photographs were sorted, selected and carefully arranged, all depicting interesting locations. The daunting task then came of elimination of many hundreds of superb subjects due to the lack of space. The next stage, the preparing of the captions to the photographs, was greatly helped by a holiday spent near the Settle and Carlisle line. Here, one obtained a special incentive when freight trains could be heard struggling up the 'long drags' of this spectacular railway. This sound and sight, amongst the most amazing scenery, seemed to portray all the air of romance and power of today's railway system, particularly when this important rail link is under a constant threat of closure. When you stop to consider the importance of this secondary through route, used particularly when any problems appear on the West Coast Main Line, then it does seem that the repair cost to maintain this route is minimal, as to its importance. There appear to be many lines all over the country in the same situation as the Settle and Carlisle line, and one only hopes that some one in Government will, one day, wake up and realize, before it is too late, that the country needs its rail system. It seems so obvious to many people that if the rail network, that is not required at present, is just left as it is, it could always be re-commissioned, if necessary, at short notice. Another strong factor that came to light, on looking through so many photographs of the railway scene, was the need to look at the feasibility of a combined freight/passenger service on the many secondary routes. The Post Office have successfully combined their collection and bus services in many parts of the country, so why not the railway? By this means, the community could be better served, with parcel/freight services being re-introduced to many areas, and lines no longer carrying passenger services now, being allowed to carry passengers once more. The use of the single railcar or a new diesel multiple unit, with larger freight carrying areas, could lead to a more cost effective system.

One last point worthy of mention, is that, by considering so many photographs of our rail system, it is apparent that our motive power is not only in short supply, but is becoming very old and tired. Many of the photographs contain scenes of 'sick' or 'dead' locomotives or the wrong motive power being used due to lack of power. Also, on the passenger front, trains seem to be getting shorter, and, on the freight service, less frequent. In all, one compiles this type of book to show the best and forward progression of our railway system, but I personally felt that, if we are not careful, soon 'Diesels Nationwide' might not be a reality any more, unless someone really cares about what Britain wants in the future from its 'primary' transport system.

I hope the content that has finally appeared within the pages of this book is a fair cross-section of the British Rail system, and that you enjoy your look at British Railways through the lenses of the contributing photographers.

Colin Judge
Oxford
April 1983

Below: A further view of the prototype unit, No. 140001 leaving Glasgow Central Station for Kilmarnock on 29th August 1981, again on passenger service evaluation trials.
Paul Shannon

Ancient and Modern

Plates 1 and 2:   These two interesting photographs show, *(Plate 1)*, the replica of the 'Rocket' being prepared, prior to the run into St. Pancras Station. It appears to have a good head of steam. The dormant Class 45 'Peak' is No. 45113. In the lower photograph, *(Plate 2)*, the 'GPO Special', with its post box visible, is about to be towed by Class 08 shunter, No. 08890 back to Cambridge Street Depot, after the ceremonies on 10th March 1980.

Brian Morrison

Plate 3 (above): Newcastle Station, on 29th May 1980, viewed from above, showing clearly the trackwork and platform layout. The activity within the photograph is quite considerable with, from left to right, an unidentified Class 03 shunter, two HST sets, Nos. 254017 and 254020, three Cravens and one Metro-Cammell diesel multiple unit, all forming services to and from Edinburgh, South Shields, Tynemouth and Sunderland.

Brian Morrison

The New Era – HSTs

Plate 4 (right): HST set, No. 254004 has its windscreen washed, on 22nd July 1980, prior to a trip to Aberdeen from King's Cross. An electric multiple unit, No. 312701, on a suburban service to Royston, stands alongside. The special type of ladder, enabling the HST screen to be cleaned, is worthy of note.

Geoff Gamble

Plate 5 (above): An Inter-City 125 in action. The 11.26 Paignton to Paddington train, with power car No 43136 leading, is seen at Dawlish Warren on 12th April 1982. This is a fine location for Western Region photography during the summer months.

Bert Wynn

Plate 6 (left): Newcastle Central Station. Pictured at this location, on 26th July 1980, is the rear end of HST set No. 254006, (power car No E43066), with a northbound train together with a diesel multiple unit comprising cars Nos. E56465 and E51204 (headed for Carlisle) waiting in the centre road. The HST set on the right of the picture is on a southbound express and is No. 254027.

Geoff Gamble

Plate 7: Driver Crunkshank, of Haymarket Depot, opens the throttle of his HST set as he starts the 'Talisman', the 16.15 Edinburgh to King's Cross Inter-City express, on 24th April 1982, from Waverley Station. Why were steam locomotives considered to be polluting the atmosphere?

Mick Howarth

Plate 8 (above): On 27th June 1979, framed by the goods shed doorway, HST set, No. 253019 propels two trailers down the gradient and rounds the curve into Lostwithiel with a Penzance to Plymouth driver training run. One of the power cars from HST set No. 253005 brings up the rear.

John Chalcraft

Plates 9 (left) and 11 (right): These two pictures clearly show the driving position and control layout of an HST power car.

Geoff Gamble

Plate 10 (above): On 22nd August 1978, the 10.10 express from Edinburgh to King's Cross, 'The Flying Scotsman', arrives at King's Cross, in the form of HST set No. 254019.

Bert Wynn

Plate 12 (left): A typical scene at Paddington Station, with two HST sets, Nos. 253027 and 253011, waiting, at 4.30p.m. on 20th August 1979, to be called for duty.

Geoff Gamble

Plate 13 (right): With power car No. 43069 leading, an HST set emerges from Mound Tunnel into a sunlit Princes Street Gardens, on departure from Edinburgh (Waverley) Station, with the 17.50 King's Cross to Aberdeen Inter-City express on 24th April 1982.

Mick Howarth

Plate 14 (above): A fine aerial view of Penwithers Junction, near Truro, on 4th July 1980, with Class 253 HST set, No. 253025, on the 10.25 Paddington to Penzance Inter-City service. The Falmouth branch can be seen going off to the left and curving away, to the right, in the trees.

Brian Morrison

Plate 15 (right): HST power cars, Nos. W43021 and W43006 rest at Paddington in August 1979. Class 47, No. 47104 awaits departure with an Inter-City express.

Andy Sparks

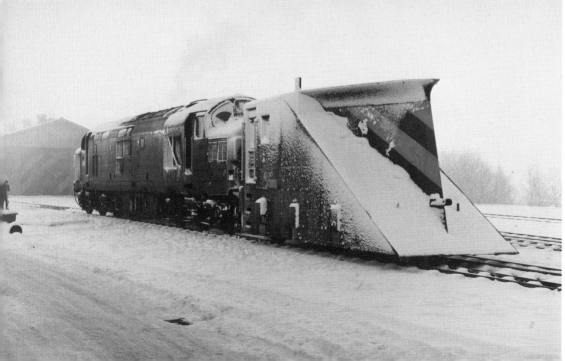

Plate 16 (above): In wintry conditions, on 12th February 1979, a Class 25/0, No. 25002, is seen, passing through Blair Atholl on a 'down' freight.

Brian Morrison

Plate 17 (left): In sub-zero conditions, on 7th January 1982, Class 37, No. 37030, complete with snowplough, waits patiently, as the shunter tries to change the points, outside the depot at Tyne Yard. The extremely severe conditions resulted in many workings being cancelled.

David Allen

In the Snow

Plate 18 (above): Class 47, No. 47525, kicks up the snow as it heads the 08.33 Hull to King's Cross service through Little Bytham on 31st December 1978.

Andrew Taylor

Plate 19 (right): A 3 car diesel multiple unit set, comprising cars Nos. M50737, M59285 and M50651, arrives at Lincoln St. Marks, on a wintry 13th February 1978, with the 07.22 ex-Crewe service.

Graham Wise

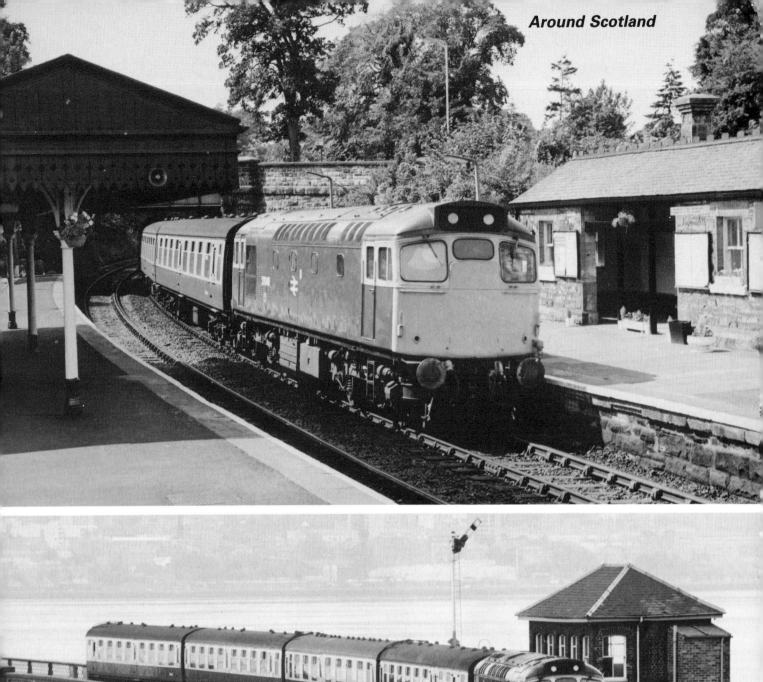

Plate 22 (above): A further Class 27 locomotive, No. 27024, leaves Markinch with the 11.21 Dundee to Edinburgh service on 11th August 1982.

Bert Wynn

Plate 23 (below): On 12th August 1982, the 16.05 (6D09) Oban to Mossend service was terminated at Crianlarich. After running round its train, Class 37, No. 37043, *Loch Lomond*, shunts the train into the sidings at Crianlarich. The vehicle next to the locomotive is condemned griddle car, No. SC1105.

Bert Wynn

Plate 20 (top left): A Class 27, No. 27040, arrives at Aberdour with the 13.17 Edinburgh to Dundee passenger service on 10th August 1982.

Bert Wynn

Plate 21 (bottom left): Seen passing Tay Bridge South signal box, with the 13.21 Dundee to Edinburgh express, is Class 27, No. 27037 on 11th August 1982.

Bert Wynn

Plate 26: With the Forth Road Bridge dominating the background, Class 27, No. 27037 approaches Inverkeithing, with the 11.17 Edinburgh to Dundee service, on 13th August 1982.

Bert Wynn

◄ *Plate 24 (top left):* Class 20 locomotives, Nos. 20217 and 20220 are seen passing Dalmeny Station, on 10th August 1982, with a southbound empty merry-go-round working. Dalmeny Station is situated at the southern end of the Forth Rail Bridge, seen in the background.

Bert Wynn

◄ *Plate 25 (bottom left):* Class 37, No. 37027, *Loch Eil*, arrives at Crianlarich with the 08.04 Glasgow to Oban train, while Class 37, No. 37111, awaits clearance with the 07.07 Corpach to Mossend freight on 12th August 1982.

Bert Wynn

Plate 27 (above): Heading the 6S41, ammonia tanks service from Haverton Hill, into Leith South Docks, on 13th August 1982, is Class 47, No. 47002. The light engine, Class 26, No. 26005, awaits clearance to return to Millerhill Depot, while an 08 shunter is busy in the yard.

Bert Wynn

Plate 28 (below): Shunting and assembling loaded china clay wagons at Wenford Bridge, Cornwall, on 3rd July 1980, is Class 08 shunter, No. 08954.

Brian Morrison

Jack of all trades – 08 Shunters

Plate 29 Class 08 shunter, No. 08233, rests at Stratford Depot on 22nd July 1977.

Fred Kerr

◀ *Plate 30 (top left):* Whilst marshalling parcels vans, on 1st May 1982, Class 08 shunter, No. 08762 moves southwards out of platform 7 at Perth Station.

David Allen

◀ *Plate 31 (bottom left):* The roundhouse at Staveley (Barrow Hill) is still used to stable locomotives. On this occasion, 7th June 1980, the access road was receiving attention and Class 08 shunters, Nos. 08196 and 08871, were stranded.

David Allen

Plate 32 (below): Performing towing duties on 24th March 1981, Class 08 shunter, No. 08424 propels Class 06 shunter, No. 06002 through Dundee Station. The Class 06 shunter had just failed whilst shunting in the docks. The shunter on the left is Class 08, No. 08761, the pilot for the upper yard.

Michael Rhodes

08771

Class	08
Weight tons	49
Brake force tons	19
RA	5
Max speed mph	15

YK

Plate 33 (above): An ex-British Rail shunter, No. 12054, now the property of A. R. Adams of Newport, is pictured at Mardy Colliery, on 10th February 1978, on hire to the National Coal Board. Notice the handmade ladder, the light on the top front and the very dubious looking track over which the engine was expected to run.

Graham Scott-Lowe

Plate 34 (left): Class 08 shunter, No. 08771, of York Depot, with its driver taking advantage of a short break in shunting to carry out some paperwork, in October 1979. Notice how the maximum speed has been changed to 15 m.p.h. by 'local' painting.

Andy Sparks

Plate 35 (right): An interesting view, full of detail, of Class 03, No. 03084 at Norwich on 29th September 1979.

Bert Wynn

Plate 36 (left): A Norwich-based shunter is used for light shunting work around Lowestoft and, between duties, is stabled in the yard, beside the station. On 1st July 1979, the chosen engine was a scruffy Class 03 shunter, No. 03029.

David Maxey

Plate 37 (below): A Class 03 shunter, No. 03189 poses at Staveley Works, in ex-works condition, on 30th January 1981.

Peter Gater

Plate 38 (right): An interesting view of Class 03 shunter, No. 03399, showing detail for the modeller, pictured at Ipswich on 15th May 1980.
John Hillmer

Master and Slave

Plate 39 (below): Tinsley's 'Master and Slave' hump shunters, Class 13, No. 13001 poses at its home depot on 14th October 1979.

Peter Gater

Plate 41 (above): Eight sails on a superb windmill, a G N R somersault signal and a station sign in a state of collapse, all make up the atmosphere of this rural scene at Heckington, as two Cravens 2 car units prepare to leave with the local service, on 10th August 1974.

Graham Wise

Plate 42 (right): As the light fails and the station takes on a new look, under its own lighting, the last train of the day from Lowestoft to Ipswich is seen here calling at Woodbridge on 17th May 1979.

John Hillmer

DMUs Countrywide

Plate 40 (left): Ilkley, still with its gas lamps, on 19th January 1980. A Metro-Cammell 2 car unit, comprising cars, Nos. E51435 and E56362 forms the 12.21 ex-Leeds and the 13.06 return service.

Brian Morrison

Plate 43 (above): New Holland Pier, on 23rd September 1978, with a 2 car diesel multiple unit, comprising cars Nos. E50046 and E56010 forming the 16.41 to Cleethorpes and, at the rear, Nos. E56007 and E50007 forming the 16.45 to Barton-on-Humber. A derelict scene with the lines on the left having been removed.

Graham Wise

Plate 44 (below): This signal box is now closed but on 30th October 1980 Arksey signal box, north of Doncaster, still had control of the passing diesel multiple unit en route for Doncaster.

Colin Marsden

Plate 45 (above): A 2 car diesel multiple unit in the attractive setting around Gargrave, between Skipton and Hellifield, on 13th May 1978.

Grenville Hounsell

Plate 46 (right): The Fakenham & Dereham Railway Society's railtour on 29th March 1980. Named the 'West Norfolk Freight Lines Railtour', it is seen here traversing the derelict King's Lynn Dock branch.

Ray King

Plate 47 (above): Having just come off the Wakefield line, a Class 101 diesel multiple unit, comprising cars Nos. E51435 and E56362, passes Goose Hill Junction, Normanton, with the 11.36 Sheffield to Leeds service on 27th May 1981.

David Allen

Plate 48 (left): Gloucester RC&W Company motor brake, 2nd single car unit, No. M55004 arrives at Stourbridge Town with the 16.40 from Stourbridge Junction on 10th August 1981. The short platform and simple shelter waiting-room do little to reflect the former glory of Stourbridge Town Station. This is one of the shorter passenger services of British Rail.

Geoff Gamble

Plate 49 (above): Leaving Tir Phil, on 15th September 1979, is a Derby Class 116 unit, with car No. W51140 leading, on the 10.08 Penarth to Rhymney service.

Brian Morrison

Plate 50 (right): The 10.30 Chester to Shrewsbury service meets an adverse signal at Croes Newydd South fork, Wrexham, while Class 25, No. 25166 makes it way to Croes Newydd stabling point on 26th March 1980.

Bert Wynn

Plate 51 (above): Leaving Bargoed, in a typical Welsh valley setting, with the 11.28 Rhymney to Penarth service, is the same 3 car unit as seen in Plate 49 but this time with car No. W51153 leading. *Brian Morrison*

Plate 52 (left): A Western Region 2 car set awaits departure from Bourne End, for Marlow, with the local service on 11th September 1981.

John Hillmer

Plate 53 (top right): Derby Class 114 unit, comprising cars Nos. E56039 and E50019, leaves Lincoln Depot and approaches Pelham Street Crossing, in preparation to take the route to Central Station, to form the 15.37 departure for Sheffield on 31st May 1980. *David Allen*

Plate 54 (bottom right): A single car unit, No. W55032, rolls into Redland, now only single line, on 11th June 1979, with the 16.23 Bristol Temple Meads to Severn Beach service.

Graham Wise

Plate 55 (above): Approaching Shildon Station, on 7th July 1980, is a Class 101, 2 car set, comprising cars Nos. E50221 and E56392, with the 10.20 Darlington to Bishop Auckland service, seen here passing the junction with the route to the now reprieved wagon works. Note the signal sighting board on the signal being passed by the train.

David Allen

Plate 56 (left): A Pressed Steel Co Class 121, motor brake second, single car unit operates the service between Maiden Newton and Bridport, on 12th April 1975, and is seen here departing from Toller Station. This branch closed on 5th May 1975 after a century or more of service to the community. Toller Station was originally opened on 31st March 1862, rebuilt in 1905, and reduced to an unstaffed halt in April 1966.

Grenville Hounsel

Plate 57 (above): An arrival at Milford Haven. A B R Swindon-built Class 120/1 unit, headed by car No. W50705, together with car Nos. W59588 and W50665, form the 11.15 Swansea to Milford Haven local service on 11th October 1979. Note the arrangements for loading and unloading, which are allowed at this station.

Brian Morrison

Plate 58 (right): On a filthy day at Manchester Victoria Station, a single car parcels unit, hauling a van, passes through the 'murk' on 20th March 1980.

John Hillmer

Plate 59 (above): Approaching Largs, on 20th January 1980, is a Derby Class 107/1 unit, with car No. SC52022 leading. The service is the 11.38 Dalry to Largs.

Brian Morrison

Plate 60 (below): A Birmingham R C & W Co. unit is pictured at King's Lynn Junction, with the 17.47 service from Ely, on 19th March 1979. The line running to the left is now a 'freight only' line.

Les Bertram

Plate 61 (right): A 2 car diesel multiple unit, forming the 11.28 Cambridge to Doncaster service, is seen passing Ely South signal box on 13th May 1980. The fine array of semaphore signals enhance the scene.

John Hillmer

Plate 62 (left): Aylesbury, on 1st February 1980, with a 4 car unit waiting to take out the 14.40 service to Marylebone.

John Hillmer

Plate 63 (right): The Rock Ferry to Helsby diesel multiple unit service, pictured at Helsby, on 6th May 1982. The two cars are Nos. M56339 and M51197. Note the differing livery styles.

John Hillmer

Plate 64 (above): Framed by the broken wire on the footbridge is a diesel multiple unit operating the Ipswich to Lowestoft service. It is seen here arriving at the rural setting of Woodbridge Station, in Suffolk, on 19th May 1979.
John Hillmer

Plate 65 (left): The outpost of Barton-on-Humber on a rainy day in March 1977, with cars Nos. E56038 and E50009 awaiting departure with the 12.37 to Cleethorpes local service.
Graham Wise

Plate 66 (right): A scene at St. Dennis Junction with the china clay mounds in the distance. The 11.40 Par to Newquay service passes, on 4th July 1980, the Western Region signalling and old GWR signal box.
Brian Morrison

Plate 67 (above): Class 31, No. 31291 and Class 37, No. 37011 stand at Ipswich on 17th May 1979.

John Hillmer

Plate 68 (above): Two faces stare out from the darkness of Birmingham New Street Station. Class 47 locomotives, Nos. 47439 (e.t.h. fitted) and 47077 *North Star*, (steam heat fitted) which is decorated for special duties.

John Chalcraft

Plate 69 (left): Class 31, No. 31406 is being prepared to haul Sir Peter Parker's train for the first sod-cutting ceremony of new Selby bypass main line scheduled for 29th July 1980. This photograph, which also shows Class 55 'Deltic', No. 55011 *The Royal Northumberland Fusiliers*, was taken at York Depot on 24th July 1980. Note the pile of brake blocks in the foreground.

Geoff Gamble

Plate 70 (left): On 15th May 1982, Class 40, No. 40060 waits to enter Holyhead container terminal with empty flat trucks.

John Hillmer

Plate 71 (above): On 19th August 1979, Class 56, No. 56064 stands in paint primer, awaiting the top coat, after construction in Doncaster Works.

Brian Morrison

Plate 72 (above): Rare stable companions. An Eastfield-allocated Class 37, No. 37149 poses beside Class 37, No. 37036 of March Depot, on the reception roads at Doncaster Works on 9th March 1980. The difference in the front ends is well portrayed in this photograph.

Peter Gater

Plate 73 (below): Front cab composition in Doncaster Works yard on 20th November 1977. Class 56 locomotives Nos. 56036 and 56037 and, in the background, Class 50, No. 50044 *Exeter*.

Peter Gater

Plate 74 (below): One of the remotest settings on British Rail. Corrour Station, in Scotland, lies on the banks of Loch Ossian in the middle of Rannoch Moor, and is inaccessible by road, serving only the station house, a shooting lodge and a youth hostel. Class 37, No. 37027 waits in the 'down' loop, for a southbound passenger train to pass, on 28th August 1981. Note the livery of the locomotive.

Paul Shannon

CORROUR

Plate 76 (right): A front cab detail portrait of Class 31, No. 31236 in King's Lynn yard on 25th August 1977. The small label on the door reads 'Expt. DL/564 — Main Generator Carbon Brush Trial'.

Geoff Gamble

20 077

31236

Plate 75 (above): Refuelling in March Depot on 16th April 1980 is Class 20, No. 20077 showing the rather unusual spacing of the numbers.

Geoff Gamble

Plate 77 (above): The 09.33 to Wolverhampton stands at Penzance, on 15th September 1979, with Class 46, No. 46021 in charge. Class 50, No. 50004 *St. Vincent* is seen backing out of platform 3, having brought in the 00.45 sleeper service from Paddington.

John Hillmer

Plate 78 (right): An unusual front portrait of an unidentified English Electric Co-Co, Type 3, Class 37, passing Class 46, No. 46015 on the Ebbw Vale line on 10th May 1975.

Grenville Hounsell

Plate 79: A selection of nameplates and numbers from British Rail locomotives.

Semaphore Signals in Modern Times

Plate 80: On 3rd October 1979, Class 31, No. 31229 approaches Ely with the 10.36 Liverpool Street to King's Lynn train. The train is running 11 minutes late, but this is still quite an achievement for a locomotive which is underpowered for this service.

John Chalcraft

Plate 81: Class 37, No. 37108 enters Crianlarich Station, on 26th August 1981, with the 13.24 Fort William (Mallaig Junction) to Sighthill air-braked freight service. This train is one of the three daily freights running, in each direction, between Glasgow and Fort William and, on this occasion, consisted mainly of empty vans from Corpach Paper Mill to Plumstead, in South London.

Paul Shannon

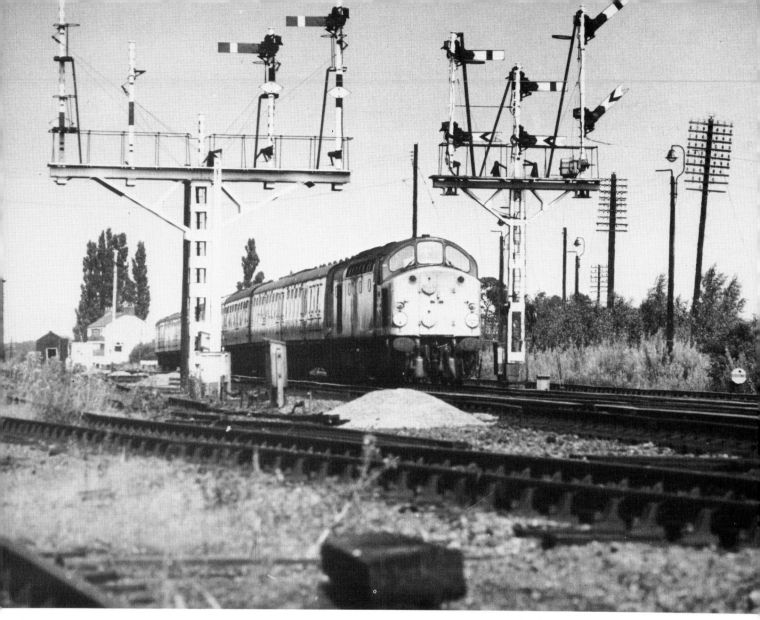

Plate 82 (above): At Pyewipe Junction, on the approach to Lincoln Central Station, in July 1976, is Class 40, No. 40121 with the 09.51 (SO) Sheffield to Skegness service. Already, the signals are disappearing from the impressive gantries seen in this picture.

Graham Wise

Plate 83 (right): Passing a selection of upper quadrant signals is a Cambridge-bound diesel multiple unit, seen here entering Ely on 13th May 1980.

John Hillmer

Plate 84: Two locomotives and two wagons! Class 31 locomotives, Nos. 31178 and 31292 take the passenger lines at Cargo Fleet, (Whitehouse Crossing) on 25th March 1982, whilst conveying bogie potash wagons from repair at Tees Shops to Tees Docks, where they will join a train of empties for the Cleveland Potash Mines at Boulby. These semaphore signals are amongst the last to survive on the Middlesbrough to Saltburn line, but rationalization is on its way and the two 'permissive block' goods lines, on the right, are soon to be taken out of use.

Paul Shannon

Plate 85 (above): On 14th March 1982, a refurbished Class 101 Metro-Cammel, 2 car set, comprising cars Nos. E56082 and E50294, approaches Stockton with the 09.20 (SuO) Newcastle to Middlesbrough service. It is pictured passing the array of semaphore signals that are a feature of the North Shore.
David Allen

Plate 86 (right): A receding view, on 14th February 1981, of a Class 101 unit as it leaves Hartlepool, on the Durham coast route, with the 12.25 Newcastle to Middlesbrough service. Normal scheduled passenger services are concentrated on the 'down' platform only.

David Allen

Plate 88 (above): A Class 110 unit, forming the 12.30 Leeds to Sheffield service, on 27th May 1981, is dwarfed by the wooden gantry on which the signals controlling the movements on the 'up' main line are displayed at Goose Hill Junction, Normanton.

David Allen

Plate 89 (right): Resting in the sidings to the east of Spalding is Class 31/4, No. 31405, having arrived earlier with an excursion (1Z70) from Guildford on 8th May 1982.

David Allen

◀ *Plate 87 (left):* Framed by the signals for Pelham Street Junction, a Lincoln-based unit, comprising cars Nos. E50015 and E56001, leaves Lincoln Central for Sleaford, at 16.07 on 19th February 1975.

Graham Wise

A class since extinct – The Deltics

Plate 90: Diverted by East Coast Main Line engineering works, the 'up' 'Flying Scotsman', the 10.00 Edinburgh to King's Cross, approaches Lincoln Central, on Sunday, 23rd April 1978, with Class 55 'Deltic' No. 55005 *The Prince of Wales's Own Regiment of Yorkshire* in charge.

Graham Wise

Plate 91 (above): Class 55 'Deltic', No. 55006 *The Fife & Forfar Yeomanry* is pictured at Doncaster, on 19th August 1979, coming off its train after hauling the 14.50 ex-Newcastle service. Many interested enthusiasts seem to be in attendance.

Brian Morrison

Plate 92 (below): One of the numerous 'Deltic' specials that ran towards the end of their life. Leaving Paddington, with the RPPR 'West Country' Special, on 19th February 1978, is Class 55 'Deltic' No. 55018 *Ballymoss.*

Brian Morrison

Plate 93: On two occasions in August 1981, Class 55 'Deltic' No. 55002 *The King's Own Yorkshire Light Infantry* made visits to the Esk Valley line. On 30th August 1981, the 'Deltic' passes through the picturesque station of Sleights with the 12.44 Whitby to Middlesbrough service.

David Allen

Plate 94 (above): Princes Street Gardens, Edinburgh, on 1st June 1977, with Class 55 'Deltic' No. 55003 *Meld* running in to take out the 16.00 service to King's Cross, London.

Brian Morrison

Plate 95 (right): The majesty of York. Haymarket-allocated Class 55 'Deltic' No. 55010 *The King's Own Scottish Borderer* arrives at York with the 11.00 King's Cross to Edinburgh service on 30th April 1977.

Peter Gater

Plate 96: The last regular 'Deltic'-hauled 'up' 'Flying Scotsman' passes Lincoln Central, on 7th May 1978, headed by Class 55 'Deltic' No. 55018 *Ballymoss*, diverted to this line by engineering works.

Graham Wise

In the Works

Plate 97 (above): Paint shop contrasts. Inside Doncaster Works, Class 55 'Deltic' No. 55006 *The Fife & Forfar Yeomanry* briefly faces *Aerolite*, in for a repaint from the National Railway Museum, on 10th June 1979.

Peter Gater

Plate 98 (below): Two generations of motive power undergoing overhaul at Derby Works on 7th June 1980. A Class 45 'Peak', No. 45017 rests alongside HST power car, No. W43024.

David Allen

Plate 99 (above):   A general view of the Diesel Repair Shop at Doncaster Works on 5th November 1978. The winter sunshine gleams through the doors and windows of the workshops.

Peter Gater

Plate 100 (left):   A refurbished Class 50, No. 50032 *Courageous* receives an early return inspection in the Diesel Repair Shop at Doncaster Works on 12th July 1981.

Peter Gater

Plate 101 (above): The end of the line for the 'Cambrian Coast Express'. The forlorn cab ends of Class 24, No. 24133, which were being cut up at Doncaster Works, lie beside the track, on 3rd September 1978.

Peter Gater

Plate 102 (below): Contrasting front ends in the Paint Shop at Doncaster Works. A Class 31, No. 31108, a newly-constructed Class 56, No. 56061 and a Class 08 shunter, No. 08401 all seen here on 10th June 1979.

Peter Gater

Plate 104 (top right): Refurbished Class 50, No. 50012 *Benbow* awaits its acceptance trials in Doncaster Works yard on ▶
10th May 1981.

Peter Gater

Plate 105 (bottom right): Class 50, No. 50048 *Dauntless* hauls a Saturday Special for the West Country, and is seen, at ▶
speed, passing through Haresfield, in Gloucestershire, on 18th July 1981.

L. J. Lennard

Plate 103 (above): A beautiful setting in Cornwall, at Bodmin Road, once an important junction station. Here, Class 50,
No. 50040 *Leviathan* leaves for Leeds with the 10.23 Inter-City service from Penzance to Leeds on 2nd July 1980. The
line just above the engine is the freight only line to Wenford Bridge.

Brian Morrison

Class 50's in Service

Plate 106 (above): Arriving at Bristol Temple Meads Station, on 19th October 1975, is Class 50, No. 50047, prior to being named *Swiftsure*, with the 16.15 empty stock train to Paddington.

Brian Morrison

Plate 107 (left): Another view of Bristol Temple Meads Station, with Class 50, No. 50018 (unnamed at this time), preparing to leave with the 09.39 to Paddington. A Class 31, No. 31241 is seen leaving with the Western Region inspection saloon, No. W80975, to Severn Beach on 26th March 1975.

Grenville Hounsell

Plate 108 (top right): Seen here, framed by the old GWR lattice bridge, is Class 50, No. 50025 *Invincible*, passing Taplow Station hauling an 'up' Inter-City express on 22nd September 1981.

John Hillmer

Plate 109 (bottom right): One of the most photographed areas on the Western Region is here at Dawlish Warren. Class 50, No. 50018 *Resolution* hauls an e.c.s train on 12th April 1982.

Bert Wynn

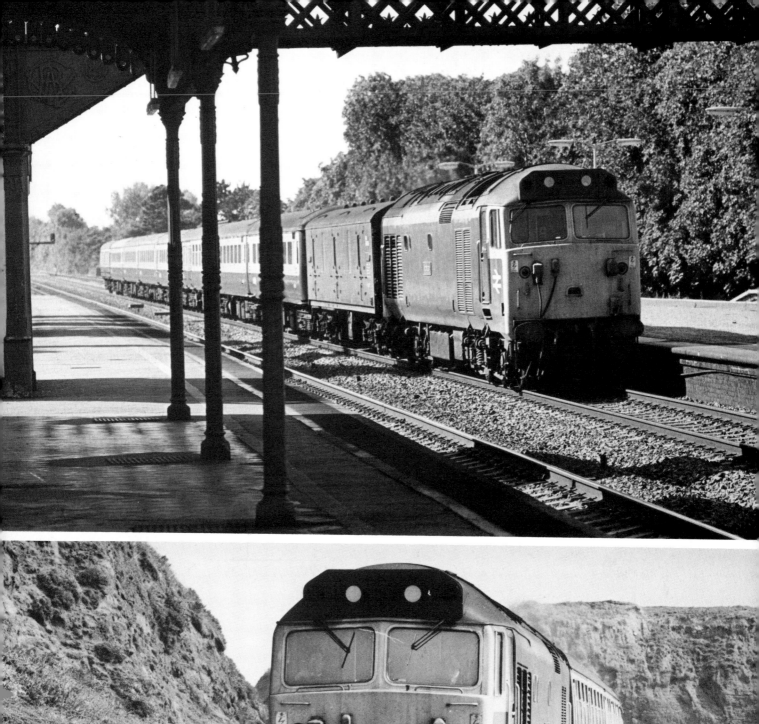

Plate 111 (above): Running back to Old Oak Common Depot for refuelling, and possible maintenance, is Class 50, No. 50009 *Conqueror* after bringing in the 16.56 Inter-City service on 20th August 1979.
Geoff Gamble

Plate 110 (top left): Class 50 locomotives are at home at Paddington, and here is a typical study of a front end of one of this class as it stands in the sunlight awaiting its crew on 14th April 1980. *Geoff Gamble*

Plate 112 (below): A fine general view of Penzance Station, on 4th July 1980, with Class 50, No. 50013 *Agincourt* coming out of the station, having arrived earlier in the day. The locomotive sports its newly-fitted spotlight. The Class 47, No. 47189, is seen at the head of the 18.08 (FO) for Leeds and the mail coaches and locomotives in the distance are of particular interest. *Brian Morrison*

Plate 113 (right): Passing Scrubs Lane Bridge, at 12.35, with a 'down' train, on 28th August 1979, is the 12.23 Paddington to Penzance express, with Class 50, No. 50035 *Ark Royal* in command.

Geoff Gamble

Plate 114 (below): On 17th April 1982, a refurbished, but grubby, Class 50 locomotive, No. 50012 *Benbow* hurries through the rather sleepy Cotswold village of Shipton under Wychwood, with the 11.46 Worcester (Shrub Hill) to Paddington train. This train has now disappeared from the 1982/83 timetable.

David Allen

Tunnels

Plate 115 (left): On 16th August 1977, Class 45 'Peak', No. 45034, with the 10.03 Newcastle to Liverpool express, emerges from Standedge Tunnel. The only water troughs ever to be located in a tunnel were situated here and, in fact, the old water tank can still be seen in the centre of the picture.

David Clough

Plate 116 (below): Copenhagen Tunnel, on 20th November 1976, with Class 55 'Deltic', No. 55006 *The Fife & Forfar Yeomanry* on the 'down' 'Flying Scotsman'. Note the tunnel and signals above the nose of the 'Deltic'.

Brian Morrison

Plates 117 and 118: Two contrasting photographs around the tunnel mouth at Ipswich Station. The top photograph *(Plate 117)* shows Class 47, No. 47569 with the Norwich to Liverpool Street express on 4th April 1982, whilst the lower photograph, *(Plate 118)* shows a Class 37, No. 37002 with the 14.24 (SX) air-braked freight service from Parkeston to Bathgate on 17th August 1978.

John Hillmer and John C. Baker

Plate 121 (above): Class 37, No. 37125 passes Swains Park open-cast coal site, on 1st April 1980, and approaches Moira West Junction, with a Doncaster Civil Engineering Department train to Cliff Hill sidings. Note the track subsidence picked out here by the telephoto lens.

Bert Wynn

Plate 122 (right): Passing Latchmere Junction, near Clapham Junction, on the West London lines, on 25th May 1977, is Brush Class 47/0, No. 47162 with an 'up' train of block tanks.

Brian Morrison

◀ Plate 119 (top left): Passing Inverness on 23rd January 1980, is an English Electric Class 40, No. 40144 with a 'down' BRT hopper train. The lines to the right go into the station whilst the building in the centre of the picture is Inverness Depot. Note the unusual position of the signal box in the 'Y' of the track system. *Brian Morrison*

◀ Plate 120 (bottom left): Exchanging the single line token at Bishop Auckland, on 27th May 1980, with Class 37, No. 37071 hauling empty wagons from Wolsingham Coal Depot. The station building, in this picture, is worthy of a glance.

Brian Morrison

Plate 124 (above): Class 31, No. 31306 on the truncated remains of the old Great Northern Railway Fens line, arrives at Bardney, from Lincoln, on 10th January 1978, with a load of coal for the sugar beet factory.

Graham Wise

Plate 125 (right): A lone Class 20 locomotive, No. 20186 hauls a very short freight near Ilkeston on 20th September 1978.

S. A. Broughton

◀ *Plate 123 (opposite):* This interesting aerial view of Newcastle Station, as seen on 29th May 1980, shows a Class 47 No. 47093 hauling an 'up' hopper train and, with a 'down' train of tank wagons, Class 37, No. 37083. A Class 102, Metro-Cammel 2 car set, with car No. E51429 leading, forms the 11.05 for Sunderland and, in the background, is the tail end of a train for Liverpool and the front end of HST set No. 254020 which has brought in the 07.32 from King's Cross.

Brian Morrison

Plate 126 (above): Manchester Victoria Station, on 1st June 1979, with a Class 25, No. 25166 passing through with a west-bound mixed freight.

John Hillmer

Plate 127 (below): On 30th March 1980, Class 47/2, No. 47290 is seen travelling north through Oxford's centre road, at speed, with a train of tank wagons. The signal box has since been demolished.

Graham Scott-Lowe

Plates 128 and 129   Seen passing Dunfermline, on 25th January 1980, is Class 20, No. 20225 with a coal train for Longannet Power Station. At the rear of the same train are two more Class 20 locomotives, Nos. 20203 and 20227, banking this heavy load of coal.

Brian Morrison

Plate 130 (above): On 18th June 1979, Class 37, No. 37269 passes Ashton Junction signal box, at the junction of Wapping Wharf and Portishead branches in Bristol, with a train of coal hoppers, and is seen heading for the main line at Parson Street Junction.

Chris Perkins

Plate 131 (left): During a period of inactivity, Class 37, No. 37070 stands astride the crossing at Seaton with an engineer's train. This freight only route to South Hetton was being relaid with long welded track when this photograph was taken on 30th June 1980.

David Allen

Plate 133 (bottom right): Kensington Olympia, on 27th January 1977, with Brush Class 47/0, No. 47005 passing from the Eastern Region on to the Southern Region, with a transfer freight train of scrap iron.

Brian Morrison

Plate 132 (top right):   Propelling two loaded ballast wagons and a brake van on to the line next to the former goods depot at Kirkby Stephen, is Class 25/2 No. 25234 on 28th March 1982. After this manoeuvre the locomotive backed on to the loaded wagons and departed for Carlisle. This Sunday engineering programme had been carried out amidst diversions from the West Coast Main Line. The signal box is of a rather interesting construction. *David Allen*

Plate 134 (left): Shunting along the old Watlington ex-GWR branch is Class 31, No. 31221 with the 10.00 cement train. It is pictured at Chinnor Cement Works sidings, in Oxfordshire, on 17th August 1979.

Geoff Gamble

Plate 135 (right): In a truly branch line setting, Class 31, No. 31322, hauling loaded wagons of wet sand, is seen leaving Middleton Towers for King's Lynn with the 13.50 train on 15th August 1979.

Geoff Gamble

Plate 136 (left): On 19th June 1979, an English Electric Class 37 locomotive passes beneath the Western Region main line, after leaving Moorswater Clay Works, on its way to Liskeard in Cornwall.

Ray King

Plate 137 (right): With a transfer freight from Whitemoor Yard to March Station goods yard, on 14th August 1979, Class 08 shunter, No. 08889 is pictured from the footbridge of March Station.

Geoff Gamble

Plate 138 (left): A further look at Chinnor Cement Works as Class 31, No. 5682, now numbered 31254, leaves Chinnor to return to Princes Risborough in August 1972.

Geoff Gamble

Plate 139 (right): Seen shunting clay wagons across the level crossing at Meledor Mill, on 21st June 1979, is Class 37, No. 37142 on this freight only branch in Cornwall.

Ray King

Plate 140 (above): On 24th August 1981, a push-pull fitted Class 27, No. 27101 leaves Dumfries Yard with a train of sliding door van fits, T.O.P.S. code 'VWV'. This type of vehicle was a 1961 development of the BR standard van which was intended to facilitate loading by fork-lift trucks but is now becoming increasingly rare and is largely limited, now, to Ministry of Defence traffic.

Paul Shannon

Plate 142 (top right): On 11th March 1980, Class 56, No. 56065 working the Welbeck Colliery to Northfleet merry-go-round service, is pictured at Glendon Junction.

Fred Kerr

Plate 143 (bottom right): Class 56 No. 56028 heads a southbound merry-go-round hopper train, and is seen here, passing through Burton upon Trent Station on 8th June 1979.

Bert Wynn

Plate 141 (above): Class 52 'Western' diesel-hydraulic locomotive, No. D1072 *Western Glory* is seen at Latteridge crossing, on 14th July 1976, with an empty stone train for Tytherington Quarry.

Graham Scott-Lowe

Further Freight Scenes

Plate 144: A train of empty merry-go-round hoppers from Fiddlers Ferry, en route to Yorkshire, is whisked towards Northenden Junction by Class 47/3 No. 47353 on 6th October 1982.

Mick Howarth

Plate 145 (above): The setting for Class 45 'Peak' locomotive, No. 45072 is the doomed Corby Works of the British Steel Corporation. Six diesel shunters, owned by the BSC, lay idle, in the background, awaiting their fate on 10th December 1979.

Graham Scott-Lowe

Plate 146 (right): A fine telephoto picture of a Class 47, No. 47245 powering round the bend beside the Kennet & Avon Canal at Froxfield Locks, on 8th April 1980, with a load of Merehead stone.

John Chalcraft

Plate 147 (left): Having arrived from Ogmore Valley Washery, on 15th April 1982, Class 37, No. 37178 propels its train into Wyndham Colliery prior to returning to the washery with a loaded train.

David Allen

Plate 148 (right): An exceptionally short goods train, with Class 24, No. 5074 (later 24074) in charge, pauses to change tokens on the Cambrian Coast line, at Llwyngwril, on 23rd May 1972.

Colin Caddy

Plate 149 (below): An immaculate Class 31/1 locomotive, No. 31285 approaches Norton East with a short freight, largely composed of tanks, bound for Tees Yard on 28th July 1982.

David Allen

Plate 150 (top right): A mixed freight is hauled away from Healey Mills Yard by a Stratford-based Class 37 locomotive, No. 37122, on 13th May 1982. On the left a sister engine heads for the yard with a train of merry-go-round hoppers.

Mick Howarth

Plate 151 (bottom right): On 14th May 1982, Class 37, No. 37210 passes through Taffs Well Station with a coal train from Stormstown to Ocean Colliery. Note the ornate Walnut Tree Junction signal box on this old Taff Vale line.

David Allen

Plate 152 (above): Class 37, No. 37230 waits at Aberbeeg with a train of mineral empties, largely composed of MDVs, bound for Rose Heyworth Colliery on 13th April 1982.

David Allen

Plate 153 (above): Class 47/0, No. 47226 emerges, on 26th February 1982, from Grinkle Tunnel with a morning train from Boulby to Teesport. This section of track was relaid when the potash mine came into production at Boulby. It follows the course of the former coast route from Middlesbrough to Whitby.

David Allen

Plate 155 (below): A train of ballast wagons is hauled towards Healey Mills by Class 37, No. 37122. The train is seen here running through the impressive Horbury Cutting, on the eastern approach to the yard, on 8th May 1982.

Mick Howarth

Plate 154 (above): Since the elimination of steam in South Wales, Class 37 locomotives have had a virtual monopoly of freight traffic in most of the valleys. Having arrived earlier at Maesteg with domestic coal, Class 37, No. 37258 heads back towards Tondu, on 15th April 1982, with mineral empties for Ogmore Valley Washery. This was the first train to run over the line for six days.

David Allen

Plate 156 (below): Class 37, No. 37170 shunts at the ABM sidings at Louth on 8th October 1979.

Graham Wise

Under the Wires

Plate 157 (left): Seen here, at Birmingham New Street, on 10th December 1979, is the light engine off the 07.00 Newcastle to Poole service, in the shape of Class 37, No. 37107.

Bert Wynn

Plate 158 (below): On 16th June 1979, Class 46 'Peak', No. 46027, with the 07.47 Penzance to Liverpool Inter-City service, is pictured at Birmingham New Street.

John Chalcraft

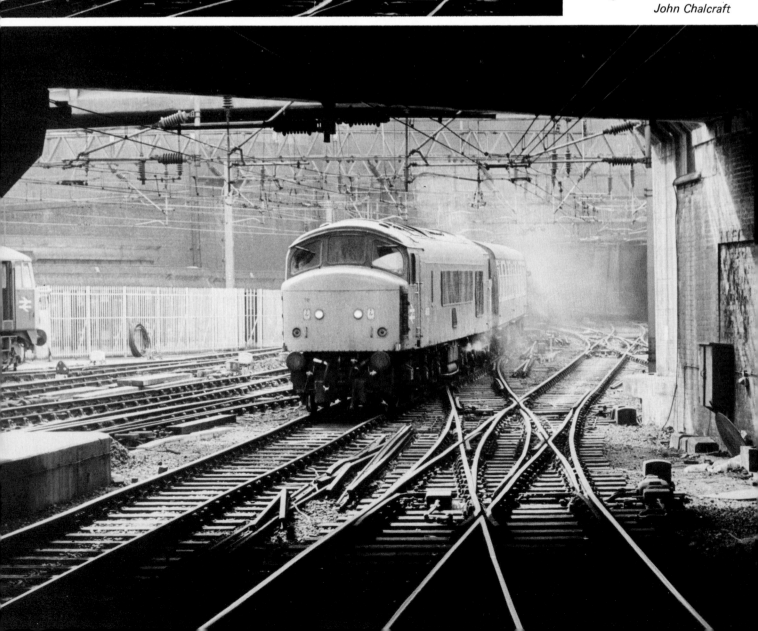

Plates 159 (above) and 160 (below):   Two views around King's Cross Station. *Plate 159* shows Class 31, No. 31203, emerging from the north end of Gasworks Tunnel, as it leaves King's Cross with an Inter-City express service. *Plate 160* shows Class 47, No. 47521 passing the stabling point, as it arrives at King's Cross, with the 10.55 from Leeds, on 6th December 1978.

John Chalcraft and Bert Wynn

Double-headers

Plate 163 (top right): Class 33, No. 33015 failed at Honiton while working the 13.00 service from Waterloo to Exeter, on 18th April 1979. Class 31, No. 31258 was summoned to assist the failed locomotive to Exeter. In this scene, the pair are descending the bank into Exeter some seventy minutes late.

Colin Marsden

Plate 161 (left): En route from Burton Depot to Coalville, after refuelling, is Class 56 No. 56035 in tandem with Class 47, No. 47366. The two locomotives are approaching Drakelow East Curve Junction on 29th June 1979.

Bert Wynn

Plate 162 (below): Two for the price of one, as Class 37 locomotives, Nos. 37094 and 37064 ease a southbound merry-go-round hopper train round the curve at Shirebrook North Junction on 12th June 1981.

Peter Gater

Plate 164: Coming off the Drinnick Mill branch, at Burngullow, near St. Austell, in Cornwall, are Class 25 locomotives, Nos. 25206 and 25012, on 2nd July 1980, with ferry vans for Carne Point.

Brian Morrison

Plate 165 (top left): On 20th June 1981, Class 20 locomotives, Nos. 20075 and 20084 enter Sleaford Station with one of the many interesting summer Saturday workings from Skegness; on this occasion the 12.58 Skegness to Derby. During 1981, the four tracks pictured here were gradually reduced to one, and the remaining sempahore signals were replaced by the inevitable colour light signals all in the interests of modernization.

Paul Shannon

◀ *Plate 166 (bottom left):* Another double-headed Class 20 working, but on this occasion the locomotives are performing their normal duty; freight haulage. Class 20 locomotives Nos. 20130 and 20133 head a northbound coal train past Shirebrook Depot on 12th June 1981. *Peter Gater*

Plate 167 (right): Having arrived earlier with the 05.50 South Tynedale Railway Society Charter from Sunderland, Class 27 locomotives, Nos. 27101 and 27102 propel some of the empty stock into Oban Station on 20th June 1981. The remainder of the train was being watered, prior to departure.

David Allen

Plate 168 (below): Kenyon Cutting, near Newton-le-Willows on Sunday, 1st June 1980, with Class 47/4, No. 47476 hauling a 'dead' Class 87/0 electric locomotive, No. 87024 *Lord of the Isles*. The train is a diverted Euston to Liverpool Inter-City express. *Brian Morrison*

Plate 169 (left): Push-pull fitted Class 47/7, No. 47712 *Lady Diana Spencer* heads the 14.00 Glasgow to Edinburgh service through Princes Street Gardens, Edinburgh, on 24th April 1982.

Mick Howarth

Passenger Services

Plate 171 (top right): Climbing out of ▶ March, with a ten coach train, on 20th June 1981, is Class 31, No. 31244 hauling the 10.15 (SO) Inter-City express from Birmingham New Street to Yarmouth.

John C. Baker

Plate 172 (bottom right): Class 31, ▶ No. 31318 passes Brandon, with its rather unique footbridge, while hauling the 09.10 (SO) express from Leeds to Yarmouth on 11th August 1979.

John C. Baker

Plate 170 (below): Class 40, No. 40159 draws gently to a halt, on 25th August 1980, at Perth, while heading the 09.50 Aberdeen to Glasgow Inter-City service. The introduction of air-conditioned stock on these services will greatly reduce the substitutions of less powerful types for the normal Class 47 locomotives.

David Allen

Plate 173 (above): Framed by the beauty of the English countryside, Class 47, No. 47125 is pictured through the trees as it passes Hewish, near Weston-super-Mare, whilst in charge of the 07.50 'Awayday' Special from Paddington to Paignton on 10th June 1979.

Chris Perkins

Plate 174 (left): Ruskington Halt, on 26th July 1975, with Class 40, No. 40012 *Aureol* passing with the 13.22 (SO) Skegness to Manchester Piccadilly service.

Graham Wise

Plate 176 (bottom right): The Spalding Flower Festival, in Lincolnshire, on Saturday, 12th May 1979, with Class 33, No. 33053 quickly removing the stock from the station, having arrived with a special from Brighton. This manoeuvre is necessary to make way for another excursion.

Andrew Taylor

Plate 175 (above): Displaced from the Glasgow to Edinburgh push-pull service, some Class 27/1 locomotives were destined to end their days based at the Inverness Depot where they are used to oust the Swindon-built diesel multiple units used on Aberdeen services. The first member of the class to be transferred was No. 27110, seen here, on 5th March 1980, heading the 08.32 Inverness to Aberdeen. It is seen at Elgin, in the passing loop, awaiting clearance of the line by a diesel multiple unit which is working an Aberdeen to Inverness service. In the background, Class 40, No. 40167, with a parcels train, awaits access to the line.

John Chalcraft

Plate 177 (above): Class 45 'Peak', No. 45126 heads the 11.50 Glasgow to Nottingham express past Methley Junction, near Castleford, on Friday, 31st March 1979.

Andrew Taylor

Plate 178 (below): The location is Weymouth Quay, with a passenger service cautiously running through the streets en route to Weymouth Quay Station. Here Class 33, No. 33109, with the 09.54 from Waterloo moves along Custom House Quay on 9th June 1979. B R officials are seen walking in front of the train to clear the route of parked cars.

Graham Wise

Plate 179: Braking hard for a stop at Swindon is Brush Class 47/0, No. 47088 *Samson*, on 24th June 1976, with the 09.00 Swansea to Paddington Inter-City service. Note the Pullman coach awaiting restoration alongside Swindon Works.

Brian Morrison

Plate 180: With the word 'olivetti' painted on the front of Class 47, No. 47508, *Great Britain*, the company-hired special departs from Waterloo, on 1st May 1979, en route to Haslemere.

Colin Marsden

Plate 181 (above): The magnificence of the scenery on the Settle and Carlisle route is superbly portrayed in this photograph. Class 47, No. 47444 is crossing Dandry Mire with the 09.15 Euston to Glasgow service on 24th April 1977. *Chris Davis*

Plate 182 (below): A further look at the Spalding Flower Festival Specials on Saturday, 12th May 1979. The trains stabled at Spalding, from left to right, are headed by Class 37, No. 37091 from Southend; Class 31, No. 31199 from King's Cross; Class 33, No. 33044 from Ramsgate; Class 31, No. 31164 from Acle and Class 33, No. 33053 from Brighton.

Andrew Taylor

Plate 183 (top right): Class 31, No. 31199 (left) stands at Skegness, on 18th July 1977, having arrived with an excursion from Sheffield. Skegness is another popular special excursion centre, and in this picture two Class 25 locomotives, Nos. 25164 and 25122, can also be seen at the head of a similar train from Burton upon Trent at platform 6. On the right of the picture Class 31, No. 31209 completes the scene.

Graham Wise

Plate 184 (bottom right): Heading east, along the Tyne Valley, through Wylam with the 1Z72 is Class 47/4, No. 47530 on a charter train from Dumfries to York, on 16th May 1982. The train is composed exclusively of Mk. I coaches and is seen passing beneath one of the two remaining overhead signal boxes in North East England.

David Allen

Plate 187 (above): Bournemouth Station, on 20th October 1979, with Class 47, No. 47121 standing with the stock for the 14.55 working to Liverpool. Alongside stands Class 33, No. 33111 waiting to be used on the local non-electrified line to Poole.

Andrew Taylor

Plate 188 (right): Class 45/0 'Peak', No. 45047, with the 09.20 Paignton to Derby express, passes the canal alongside the University of Birmingham on 16th June 1979.

Graham Scott-Lowe

Plate 185 (top left): Newly re-liveried in Scottish style, Class 37, No. 37112 crosses the River Lochy, between Fort William and Banavie, with the 16.30 Fort William to Mallaig service, on 27th August 1981. This working is still officially 'mixed traffic' and occasionally carries fuel oil tanks for Mallaig.

Paul Shannon

Plate 186 (bottom left): This busy scene portrays a great deal of activity north of Leicester Station on 15th June 1981. Class 45 'Peak', No. 45118 departs with a northbound express, whilst arriving on a Norwich to Birmingham working is Class 31, No. 31241. Standing with a CCE train for Croft, on the Leicester to Nuneaton line, is Class 31, No. 31187.

Paul Shannon

◀ *Plate 189 (top left):* Arriving at Pitlochry, on 22nd January 1980, with the 08.15 Inverness to Glasgow Queen Street express, is Brush Class 47/0, No. 47120. The station furniture and bridge are typical of those to be found in the Scottish Highlands.

Brian Morrison

◀ *Plate 190 (bottom left):* Due to engineering works at Stalybridge, on 6th April 1980, a Liverpool to Scarborough train, headed by Class 47, No. 47532, approaches Todmorden.

John Chalcraft

Plate 191 (right): A typically bleak, wet and windy day at Blea Moor, on 30th January 1982, with an unidentified Class 47 locomotive in charge of a 'down' train of long wheelbase oil tanks, placed into the loop to let Class 47/0, No. 47105 pass with an excursion from Sheffield to Carlisle.

David Allen

Plate 192 (below): Throughout the winter 1981/82 timetable, many West Coast Main Line Anglo-Scottish services were diverted, on Sundays, via the Settle and Carlisle line. Class 47/4, No. 47484 *Isambard Kingdom Brunel*, sporting a 'GB' sticker, passes through the 'Dalesrail' Kirkby Stephen Station, on 28th March 1982, with the 10.40 Glasgow (Central) to Euston Inter-City service.

David Allen

Plates 195 and 196 (opposite): Two famous locomotive types, both now extinct on British Rail, are pictured at Paddington during their working lives. *Plate 195* shows Class 55 'Deltic' No. 55018 *Ballymoss* on a RPPR Special and *Plate 196* shows a Class 52 'Western' diesel-hydraulic locomotive, *Western Viscount*, returning light engine to Old Oak Common Depot.

Brian Morrison and Geoff Gamble

Around Paddington

Plate 193 (left): A line up at the stop blocks, at the famous London terminus of Paddington, at 16.05 on 20th August 1979, includes Class 47, No. 47171, Class 50, No. 50012 *Benbow* and two HST units.

Geoff Gamble

Plate 194 (below): Having just hauled in the empty coaching stock from Old Oak Common Depot, two Class 31 locomotives stand 'dead' at the buffers on 19th February 1979. The locomotives are Nos. 31415 and 31412, both Old Oak Common-based.

Brian Morrison

Plate 199 (above): From a high vantage point overlooking Ranelagh Bridge stabling point, just outside Paddington, a 'down' parcels train is seen pulling away from the parcels bay, on 25th April 1973, behind Brush Class 31/2, No. 5842, later renumbered 31416. *Brian Morrison*

Plate 200 (right): The 11.32 ex-Swansea arrives at Paddington, on 21st May 1975, with a 'dead' Class 47 locomotive, No. 47509 being piloted by Class 47, No. 47070. This train is running very late indeed. *Brian Morrison*

Plate 197 (top left): Waiting for the 'off' at Paddington, on 25th February 1978, is HST unit No. 253009 and Class 50, No. 50016. The HST forms the 12.15 service to Swansea and the Class 50 the 12.30 working to Paington. *Brian Morrison*

Plate 198 (bottom left): A fine low level photograph of a Class 50 locomotive, No. 50019, later named *Ramillies*, on 9th August 1977, with the 13.30 Paddington to Penzance Inter-City service. *Brian Morrison*

Solos

Plate 205 (above): Formerly British Thomson-Houston Type 1 Bo-Bo locomotive, No. D8243, and built in 1957, this locomotive has been converted to a stationary carriage heating unit and renumbered ADB968000. This engine was repainted, it is believed, at Colchester, during March 1979, in the lighter of the two greens originally applied to Class 47 locomotives when new. It is pictured at Stratford on 8th April 1979.

David Maxey

Plate 206 (left): On 15th May 1979, two Class 20 locomotives, Nos. 20152 and 20182 head through Burton upon Trent with Class 56, No. 56039 in tow.

Bert Wynn

Plate 207 (top right): On the depot at Shirebrook, awaiting its next duty, is Class 56, No. 56086, on 22nd March 1981.

Peter Gater

Plate 208 (bottom right): An immaculate Class 08 shunter, No. 08142 poses at Toton Depot on 22nd March 1980.

Peter Gater

Plate 209 (above): Class 50, No. 50011 *Centurion* rests, at Plymouth Station, before departing with an Inter-City express.

South Devon Railway Museum

Stationary

Plate 210 (below): A York-allocated Class 47 locomotive, No. 47522, poses, in immaculate condition, at Tinsley Depot on 20th July 1980, having worked a Royal Train duty on the previous day.

Peter Gater

Plate 211 (above): Knottingley (KY) Depot, on 10th February 1979, with a host of engines on shed. Many engines have been left with their engines running over the weekend. They include Class 47 locomotives, Nos. 47316, 47373, 47277, 47375 and 47308.

Brian Morrison

Sheds and Stabling Points

Plate 214 (above): A line up at Stratford (SF) Depot with Class 31/1, No. 31002 and various Class 47 loco-motives, headed by No. 47102, waiting to return to duty.

Norman Preedy

Plate 215 (right): A Class 25, No. 25198 stands near the refuelling point at Buxton Depot on 4th May 1980.

John Hillmer

◄ *Plate 212 (top left):* Ipswich Station stabling point, on 20th April 1975, with Class 03 shunters, Nos. 03160 and 03032 and Class 31 locomotives, Nos. 31221 and 31177 waiting to be called for duty.

Norman Preedy

◄ *Plate 213 (bottom left):* On 20th July 1975, Finsbury Park Depot is pictured with Class 55 'Deltic' locomo-tive, No. 55021 *Argyll & Sutherland Highlander* standing outside the workshops.

Graham Scott-Lowe

Plate 216: Class 37 locomotives, including Nos. 37036 and 37017, stand in line at Stratford (SF) Depot on 13th November 1977.

Graham Scott-Lowe

Plate 217 (left): A British Rail Class 08 shunter, No. 08760 and Birmingham RC&W Class 33/1, No. 33118 stand at Eastleigh Depot on 11th February 1978. Both locomotives are dual braked and the Class 33/1 is fitted for push-pull working with multiple unit stock.

Grenville Hounsell

Plate 218 (above): During 1964, the 'Peak' class of locomotive commenced service on the 'Pines Express' into Bath Green Park. This entailed a local Bath to Bristol trip for refuelling purposes. On 7th May 1965, Class 45, No. D13, now renumbered 45001, passes Barrow Road Depot on its approach to Bristol on such a trip.

John Chalcraft

Back in the Good Old Days!

Plate 219 (right): On 5th March 1967, the last day of through passenger working between Birkenhead and Paddington, Class 47, No. D1636, now renumbered 47482, leaves Ruabon with one of the last Birkenhead to Paddington services.

Bert Wynn

Plate 220 (above): Class 47, No. 1863, now renumbered 47213, rounds the curve through Lincoln St. Marks, on 16th April 1973, with an iron-ore tipper train from High Dyke to Scunthorpe. Rationalization has seen the removal of the signals and signal box and has resulted in drastic track alterations.
Graham Wise

Plate 221 (left): The Class 35 'Hymeks' pictured, when new, at Swindon, having just been delivered from Beyer Peacock & Co. in 1963. Locomotives visible are Nos. D7049 and D7051 and are outside the 'A' shop.

B. D. Coldwell

Plate 222 (bottom left): On a fast run and passing Shrivenham signal box with a good load, in 1963, is another 'Hymek', No. D7017, which is now preserved.

B. D. Coldwell

Plate 223 (above): Coming off a northbound service, at Doncaster, in August 1972, is Class 55 'Deltic', No. 9004 *Queen's Own Highlander*, now renumbered 55004. Class 47, No, 1500, now renumbered 47401, waits to take over the train.
Bert Wynn

Plate 224 (right): 'Warship' Class, No. D867 *Zenith* is seen together with another unidentified member of the class, in 1968, at Swindon Works.

B. D. Coldwell

Plate 225 (below): An unidentified Class 35 'Hymek' locomotive is seen here, at Paddington, en route for Old Oak Common Depot.
Graham Wareham

Plate 226 (above): Swindon-built 'Warship' class, Type 4, B-B diesel-hydraulic locomotive, No. D824 *Highflyer* has just been attached to the Brighton to Plymouth train at Salisbury, on Thursday, 30th July 1964, and is a replacement for Class 33, No. D6500.

Grenville Hounsell

Plate 227 (left): Class 26, No. D5301, now renumbered 26001, is pictured, on 28th March 1964, at Carlisle heading a late arrival from Edinburgh.

John Whiteley

Plate 228 (above): Experimental locomotive No. 1200, *Falcon*, seen here arriving at Bristol Temple Meads with a train from Paddington on 11th July 1972.

Bert Wynn

Plate 229 (right): Heading an empty stock working up Holloway Bank, out of the King's Cross complex, in August 1962, is British Thomson-Houston, Type 1 Bo-Bo locomotive, No. D8238.

Brian Morrison

Plate 230 (above): Keeping good company with Class 24, No. D5059, later renumbered 24059, at Croes Newydd Depot, Wrexham, in 1967, are Class 40 locomotives, Nos. 269 and D374, later renumbered 40069 and 40174 respectively.

Bert Wynn

Plate 231 (left): Brand new and on a running-in turn, in 1961, is Class 55 'Deltic', No. D9003 *Meld* later renumbered 55003 and it is also in the two-tone green livery.

British Rail

Plate 232: Awaiting the 'right away' from Doncaster Station is Class 47, No. 1774. This locomotive was first renumbered 47179 and later 47577. It is pictured, in August 1972, with a southbound service (1A28) from Doncaster and the two-tone green livery is clearly visible.

Bert Wynn

Plate 233: At Croes Newydd Depot, Wrexham, in 1967, a Class 40, No. D255, later renumbered 40055, passes a line of withdrawn Standard Class 4 steam locomotives signifying the change of the times.

Bert Wynn

Plate 234: As the sun sets, an English Electric Class 40 locomotive, No. 40119 passes Wigan with an 'up' train of tank wagons on 23rd September 1976.

Brian Morrison